Hal•Leonard Instrumental Play-Along

AUDIO ACCESS INCLUDED

PLAYBACK+
Speed • Pitch • Balance • Loop

FLUTE

Disney · PIXAR
COCO

Audio arrangements by Peter Deneff

To access audio visit:
www.halleonard.com/mylibrary
Enter Code
7236-4516-0477-9376

ISBN 978-1-5400-2133-5

HAL•LEONARD®
7777 W. BLUEMOUND RD. P.O. BOX 13819 MILWAUKEE, WI 53213

In Australia Contact:
Hal Leonard Australia Pty. Ltd.
4 Lentara Court
Cheltenham, Victoria, 3192 Australia
Email: ausadmin@halleonard.com.au

Visit Hal Leonard Online at
www.halleonard.com

EVERYONE KNOWS JUANITA
from COCO

Flute

Music by GERMAINE FRANCO
Lyrics by ADRIAN MOLINA

rit.

MUCH NEEDED ADVICE
from COCO

Flute

Music by MICHAEL GIACCHINO
and GERMAINE FRANCO
Lyrics by ADRIAN MOLINA

LA LLORONA
from COCO

FLUTE

Traditional Mexican Folksong
Arranged by GERMAINE FRANCO

PROUD CORAZÓN

from COCO

FLUTE

Music by GERMAINE FRANCO
Lyrics by ADRIAN MOLINA

REMEMBER ME
(Ernesto de la Cruz)
from COCO

Words and Music by KRISTEN ANDERSON-LOPEZ
and ROBERT LOPEZ

Flute

UN POCO LOCO
from COCO

Flute

Music by GERMAINE FRANCO
Lyrics by ADRIAN MOLINA

THE WORLD ES MI FAMILIA

from COCO

FLUTE

Music by GERMAINE FRANCO
Lyrics by ADRIAN MOLINA